SUMMARY[*]

Reports from the twelve Federal Reserve Districts indicate that economic activity continued to expand across most regions and sectors from early January through mid-February. Six Districts noted that the local economy expanded at a moderate pace since the prior reporting period. Activity rose modestly in Philadelphia and Cleveland, while it increased slightly in Kansas City. Dallas noted a similar pace of growth as in the previous period, while Richmond reported that activity slowed from the modest pace seen in the prior period. Boston noted that business contacts were fairly upbeat this period, notwithstanding the severe weather.

Consumer spending rose in most Districts, and contacts were generally optimistic about near-term sales. Travel and tourism also increased in the reporting Districts. Manufacturing generally posted gains across the Districts, although at varying rates. The demand for nonfinancial services also grew moderately on balance. Home sales increased in most Districts, while reports on residential construction were mixed. Commercial real estate market conditions remained stable or improved across the Districts. Banking conditions generally improved, and credit quality remained largely unchanged. Agricultural conditions generally worsened, and oil and natural gas drilling declined.

Payrolls remained stable or expanded across the Districts, and contacts noted employment gains in a broad range of sectors. Wage pressures remained moderate and were limited largely to workers in skilled occupations. Most District contacts cited only flat to slightly increasing prices.

---

[*] Prepared at the Federal Reserve Bank of St. Louis and based on information collected on or before February 23, 2015. This document summarizes comments received from business and other contacts outside the Federal Reserve System and is not a commentary on the views of Federal Reserve officials.

Consumer Spending and Tourism

Most Districts reported that overall consumer spending increased during the reporting period. The Kansas City District, however, reported that retail sales had declined since the previous survey, but were unchanged from one year ago. The Minneapolis, Atlanta, Kansas City, and San Francisco Districts reported growth in restaurant sales. Among retailers, the outlook was generally optimistic in the Philadelphia, Cleveland, Atlanta, Kansas City, and San Francisco Districts. Both the New York and Boston Districts reported that harsh winter weather negatively affected retail business in their Districts; however, the Boston and Cleveland Districts also reported increased sales of winter-related items such as winter apparel, rock salt, and snow shovels. The Minneapolis District noted that some apparel stores had difficulty selling winter clothing due to a relatively mild winter in December and January.

Automobile sales rose in most Districts during the reporting period. The Richmond District reported that sales of cars and light trucks were flat. Reports from the Atlanta, Cleveland, Chicago, Kansas City, and San Francisco Districts indicated increased demand for trucks or SUVs. The New York, Cleveland, and St. Louis Districts noted higher sales of new vehicles during the reporting period. The Philadelphia, Kansas City, and Dallas Districts expressed optimistic outlooks for future automobile sales.

Travel and tourism improved in the New York, Philadelphia, Atlanta, Kansas City, and San Francisco Districts. The Richmond District reported a typical seasonal slowdown in activity. The New York District noted that tourism has remained robust in recent weeks. The Philadelphia District noted that ski season tourism has grown at a healthy pace, similar to that of last year's good season. The Minneapolis District indicated that winter tourism was mixed.

Manufacturing and Other Business Activity

Manufacturing generally increased since the previous survey, although the rate of growth varied across the Districts and sectors. The Atlanta District noted that manufacturing rebounded during the current reporting period following a modest slowdown in December. According to contacts in the Chicago and San Francisco manufacturing rose moderately, while contacts in New York noted modest gains. Contacts in Kansas City indicated slow growth, contacts in Philadelphia reported slight increases, and contacts in Dallas noted flat to positive growth. Reports from factory contacts in Cleveland District were mixed, while contacts in Richmond noted that activity weakened. Manufacturers had generally positive outlooks going forward. Firms in Atlanta expect production levels to increase over the next three to six months, some firms in Chicago expect steady growth in shipments for 2015. Manufacturers in Boston, Cleveland, and Richmond reported positive outlooks. In contrast, New York District contacts have grown less optimistic about the near-term outlook.

Automobile manufacturing output rose in the Cleveland, Chicago, and St. Louis Districts. Aerospace manufacturers in San Francisco expect 2015 to be a record year, and aerospace manufacturers in St. Louis reported plans to expand. Reports from primary and fabricated metals manufacturers were mixed. Firms in Chicago reported steady gains in new orders, firms in Dallas reported slower growth in demand, and firms in Philadelphia, St. Louis, and Kansas City reported weakness. In Cleveland, shipments for steel were softer than expected. Contacts in Cleveland, Chicago, and San Francisco cited increased competition from imports as a constraining factor for steel manufacturing. Industrial equipment manufacturing was mixed in Richmond and Dallas, while the Philadelphia, Chicago, and Minneapolis Districts reported gains in activity. Kansas City and San Francisco reported slower growth in machinery production.

Electrical equipment manufacturers in Richmond reported no change in shipments and orders from the previous report, while contacts in Kansas City noted slower growth in electronics. Contacts in Philadelphia and Dallas reported an increase in the demand for electronic devices. Healthcare device manufacturers in Richmond noted reduced sales. Chemical producers in the Dallas District noted declining export demand and decreased refinery utilization rates, while chemical manufacturers in St. Louis announced plans to hire additional employees and expand operations. Food producers in Richmond, Kansas City, and Dallas noted increases in demand.

Nonfinancial service activity increased in Philadelphia, Richmond, St. Louis, and Kansas City, and San Francisco. New York and Minneapolis noted an increase in activity at professional business firms. Demand for information technology services generally improved, with increases in activity cited in Minneapolis and Kansas City. However, firms in Boston noted that good business conditions were tempered by weakness abroad and firms in New York noted some weakening. Healthcare services utilization was mixed to slightly positive. Contacts in Boston, Cleveland, and St. Louis noted increasing demand for labor in healthcare, contacts in New York reported stable activity, and contacts in San Francisco noted mixed demand. Transportation demand generally improved. Contacts in Kansas City and New York noted increases in activity. Contacts in Atlanta and Philadelphia cited record shipping volume. Contacts in Cleveland and Richmond indicated that shipping volume has remained strong since the previous report. Contacts in Atlanta noted that disruptions at West Coast ports may be contributing to the increase in shipping volume. Drilling service firms in Minneapolis reported reduced demand due to lower oil prices, and oilfield services contacts in Dallas noted a sharp decline in demand.

Real Estate and Construction

Residential real estate conditions were mixed across the Districts. Home sales and prices increased in most Districts; construction activity was mixed, with some Districts reporting disruptions due to severe weather. Residential sales increased in Boston, Philadelphia, Richmond, St. Louis, Dallas, and San Francisco. Sales fell in Cleveland and Kansas City. Contacts in New York, Philadelphia, and Cleveland partially attributed lower construction to inclement weather conditions. Contacts in Boston noted low levels of inventory due, in part, to inclement weather. Reports noted that low levels of inventory and lack of desirable lots continue to slow the market: Contacts in Boston, Cleveland, Kansas City, and San Francisco cited a lack of available inventory, while contacts in Cleveland and Richmond noted a lack of available lots. Single-family building permits increased in St. Louis and San Francisco. Contacts in Cleveland, Atlanta, Kansas City, and Minneapolis reported flat to declining real estate construction.

Commercial real estate market conditions were stable or improving in most Districts. Commercial vacancy rates declined in Boston, Chicago, St. Louis, and Kansas City. In Dallas, contacts reported that commercial real estate had steadied or slowed since the previous report. The apartment market remained strong in most Districts. Apartment rental rates rose in New York, Chicago, and San Francisco. Contacts in Cleveland noted an increased demand for multifamily housing. Contacts in Dallas noted that apartment demand remains strong. Commercial construction increased in most Districts. Contacts in New York, Richmond, Atlanta, St. Louis, and San Francisco noted stable to strong multifamily construction. Contacts in Chicago reported moderate growth in commercial real estate, driven mainly by industrial buildings. In Boston, contacts noted that speculative construction remains limited due to high construction costs.

Banking and Finance

Reports on banking conditions were mostly positive across the Districts. Overall loan demand increased in all reporting Districts, with the exception of Kansas City, where loan demand was mixed. Reports on the pace of increase varied from slight in Richmond and Dallas to strong in Atlanta and New York. Commercial real estate loan demand was strong in Philadelphia and Cleveland. Commercial loan demand increased in New York, was particularly strong in Cleveland and Atlanta, was steady in Kansas City, and was mixed in Richmond. Residential lending was positive at all reporting banks, with bankers in Cleveland, Richmond, Chicago, and San Francisco noting an increase in refinancing activity.

Reports across the Districts indicated that credit quality has remained largely unchanged or has improved since the prior reporting period. Bankers in most Districts reported no change in their own lending standards. However, several bankers in the Richmond and St. Louis Districts reported relaxed standards. Bankers in the Philadelphia, Richmond, and San Francisco Districts noted that competition is lowering lending standards more generally.

Agriculture and Natural Resources

Agricultural conditions worsened since the previous report across the Districts due to weak farm income, persistent drought, and declining exports. Prices for corn and soybeans fell over the reporting period in the Chicago, Kansas City, and Dallas Districts. A majority of contacts in the Minneapolis and Kansas City Districts noted that farm incomes had fallen from year-earlier levels. Kansas City noted that farmland values had leveled off after recent gains while ranchland values continued to rise due to strong demand. Input prices for the upcoming spring planting season were reported as stable in the Richmond and Chicago Districts. Contacts in the Dallas and San Francisco Districts noted that a stronger dollar was hurting agricultural exports. Furthermore, the Chicago and San Francisco Districts noted that labor disputes at ports along the West Coast have also had a negative impact on exports. Drought conditions improved but still persisted in some areas of the Atlanta and Dallas Districts, while drought conditions in the San Francisco District hurt yields and didn't show immediate signs of improvement.

Oil and natural gas drilling declined in the Cleveland, Minneapolis, Kansas City, and Dallas Districts. In contrast, the Richmond District reported that natural gas production was unchanged. The number of drilling rigs for oil and natural gas declined sharply in the Cleveland, Minneapolis, and Kansas City Districts. Oil and gas producers in the Cleveland, Kansas City, and Dallas Districts anticipate cuts in capital expenditures during 2015. Coal production was unchanged in both the Cleveland and Richmond Districts, while it increased modestly in the St. Louis District. Both the Cleveland and Richmond Districts reported lower coal prices.

Employment, Wages, and Prices

Employment levels remained stable or continued to grow in most Districts and across a variety of sectors. Contacts in several Districts noted strong labor demand and challenges filling a variety of skilled positions. Firms in the Philadelphia District reported positive employment trends in a broad range of sectors, with the majority of hires due to economic growth rather than replacement. Businesses in the New York District continued to increase employment. Contacts in the Boston and Cleveland Districts reported little change in hiring. The Cleveland, Atlanta, Richmond, and Dallas Districts reported increased hiring in manufacturing. In contrast, contacts in the gas and oil production and related industries in the Cleveland, Atlanta, Minneapolis, Kansas City, and Dallas Districts reported downsizing or layoffs.

Wage pressures were moderate across most Districts, but some contacts reported increased wages to attract skilled workers for difficult-to-fill positions. In particular, service sector firms in the New York District noted increasingly widespread reports of wage hikes. Contacts in the Cleveland, Richmond, and Kansas City Districts noted increased wage pressure due to the difficulty in attracting and retaining truck drivers. A staffing firm in the Chicago District reported some companies were also willing to raise rates for unskilled workers to reduce turnover, and contacts in the Atlanta District noted increasing entry-level wages.

Most Districts reported flat to slight increases in overall prices. Contacts in the Cleveland and San Francisco Districts noted lower fuel surcharges, but contacts in the Atlanta and San Francisco Districts also remarked that the decline in energy prices was seen mainly as an opportunity for businesses to improve margins. The Cleveland, Chicago, and San Francisco Districts indicated that prices of some construction materials rose during the reporting period. The Kansas City District cited modest increases in retail prices, and the Dallas District noted steady prices. Manufacturing firms in the Richmond and Kansas City Districts reported that their input costs climbed at a slower pace, whereas those in the Dallas District noted they were flat to lower. Transportation contacts in the Chicago District reported that shipping costs were pushed up due to delays at West Coast ports.

FIRST DISTRICT – BOSTON

Business contacts in the First District are fairly upbeat this round, notwithstanding selective negative impacts from unseasonably severe weather in southern New England. Most responding retailers and all contacted manufacturers report sales growth from a year earlier; software and information technology services firms also cite revenue increases, and residential real estate contacts say December was strong. By contrast, staffing firms have seen business activity fall off because of weather closures, and residential real estate markets are said to have softened in early 2015 because of the inclement weather. Commercial real estate markets remain mostly solid in the region. Labor markets are largely unchanged, as most business contacts are doing minimal hiring; nonetheless, staffing firms cite inadequate labor supply as their main challenge. Pricing is not generally noted as an issue, except for some manufacturers' concerns with the strong dollar. The outlook among contacted First District firms is largely positive across major sectors.

Retail and Tourism

First District retail respondents report that their comparable-store sales have ranged from flat to up 18 percent on a year-over-year basis; however, the most frequently cited increases were between 3.5 percent and 5.5 percent. Footwear, outerwear, activewear, and winter sporting goods are selling particularly well. The firm reporting the 18 percent increase attributes about three-quarters of the added volume to strong demand for winter-related items like rock salt and snow shovels, as the Boston area and other parts of New England experienced record snowfalls between mid-January and mid-February. Other contacts say that early 2015 sales continued the positive trajectory in place by the end of 2014, but business dropped off noticeably in late January, when the first of four (to date) significant winter storms hit. One retailer reports that over the last month, about 200 of their stores based in New England had been closed for a few days because of the severe weather.

Contacts report that inventories are being actively managed; some deliberately increased stock by taking advantage of wholesale deals that suppliers offered at the end of 2014, while others plan to do some strategic trimming of inventory over the next 6 to 12 months. Most contacts report having fairly aggressive capital spending plans for 2015; investment is targeted toward information technology plus opening new stores and/or renovating or relocating existing stores. These plans are a reflection of expected continual improvement in general economic conditions, improved consumer sentiment, and hence a better retail environment. During the last few years, one contact has continually maintained a "sideways" (flat) outlook for the U.S. economy, but on this round reports that in 2014:Q4 his firm saw the first consistent week-to-week improvement in sales in several years; as a result, he is upgrading his forecast to "better."

Manufacturing and Related Services

All nine manufacturing firms contacted this cycle report higher sales versus the same period a year earlier. The main headwind they cite is the strong dollar. As a contact in the tool business explained, higher exchange rates have both "transactional costs" which are lost sales due to higher costs, and "translational costs" which result simply from the fact that income denominated in foreign currencies comes in lower when translated into dollars. Two respondents said exchange rates were a first-order problem. For the tool-maker, both translational and transactional costs are issues. For a maker of computer storage devices, the costs appear to be largely translational and are said to be more of a problem for its investors than for its U.S. production and employment.

Of the firms that report inventory, only one cites a significant change; inventories are down, but for reasons of efficiency, not cyclical factors. Other than those expressing concern about exchange rates, only one firm reports a pricing issue. A dairy producer says that its 8 percent increase in sales is entirely due to higher prices: sales by physical volume remain exactly the same; because there was a corresponding increase in costs, profits did not change.

All responding firms report stable or rising employment, but only one firm, a manufacturer of health-care devices, says it is increasing employment substantially, adding about 3 percent to staff each quarter. Even firms with very strong sales growth seem hesitant to hire. For example, a maker of fitness equipment reports 16 percent higher sales in the fourth quarter of 2014 compared to a year earlier but is waiting until the second half of 2015 to see if sales growth continues before adding to headcount. Capital investment is up at all contacted firms. However, none report major revisions to investment plans.

The outlook is positive for all manufacturing respondents. One contact at a semiconductor-related firm says sales are expected to be down in 2015 from a strong 2014, and attributes the softness to long cycles in the semiconductor business, which do not follow the standard business cycle.

Software and Information Technology Services

New England software and information technology services contacts generally report good business conditions in recent months, with year-over-year revenue increases ranging from 1 percent to 14 percent. Contacts add that growth was somewhat tempered by weakness in Europe and Asia, and a slight contraction in customer expenditures in the fourth quarter of 2014. Selling prices have generally remained stable, although one firm is escalating renewal prices modestly. While most firms have maintained current wages, one contact noted upward pressure on salaries. Capital and technology spending has largely remained constant in recent months. The majority of firms increased headcount through acquisitions and increased utilization of contractors. One firm reduced headcount to offset the previous quarter's expansion from mergers and acquisitions. Looking forward, contacts are either slightly less optimistic or maintain the same level of optimism as when we last spoke three months ago. While most firms expect high single-digit year-over-year revenue increases in the first few months of 2015, one firm anticipates revenues to be down year-over-year because of the effects of the appreciation of the dollar on their earnings in Europe and Asia. Some respondents continue to express concerns about the overall macroeconomy.

Staffing Services

First District staffing contacts report softened business activity in recent months, which they attribute to inclement weather throughout the region. Most firms report year-over-year revenue declines in the high single-digit to low double-digit range. Only one firm's revenues were up year-over-year at the end of January; however, the firm expects February revenues to be down substantially. In general, labor demand continues to be strong, with increases for a variety of positions in the healthcare, maintenance work, IT, legal, and sales sectors. Labor supply reportedly continues to be a challenge across all industries, with one firm noting particular difficulties in filling clerical and assembly roles. Firms' strategies to attract candidates continued to include print advertising, online recruiting, networking, and social media outreach. Reports on billing and pay rates are mixed; some firms report low single-digit increases in both rates, while others report no changes. Looking forward, contacts generally maintain a steady level of "cautious optimism." Despite a sluggish start to the year, contacts hope for single-digit to low double-digit year-over-year revenue growth as the weather improves. The main factors expected to affect business in the upcoming months include health insurance costs from the Affordable Care Act, continued weather-related closures, and difficulties in recruiting candidates to meet client demand.

Commercial Real Estate

Across the First District, commercial real estate markets are seen as either steady or improving. According to contacts, the harsh winter weather in the District is affecting retail activity and business productivity in the short run, but is not having significant effects on commercial real estate leasing and sales activity. One contact reports that some office landlords in downtown Hartford are posting higher asking rents for the first time in years. While tenants in greater Hartford appear increasingly to favor downtown locations, it is reportedly too soon to tell whether they will be willing to pay the higher asking rents. Sales activity for commercial properties in Connecticut remains solid while construction activity is minimal. Reports from Boston contacts remain very positive. The city's commercial properties (as well as its multifamily structures) continue to be in very high demand among foreign investors especially, who reportedly rank Boston among the top five commercial real estate markets worldwide. Office rents are seeing significant growth in top neighborhoods as vacancy rates continue to edge down thanks to business expansion and lack of new supply. Despite the tight office market in greater Boston, speculative office construction remains very limited, according to contacts, because construction costs are too high in relation to expected rents; still, build-to-suit office construction continues at a modest pace. Also in greater Boston, a lender to commercial real estate extended a few new loans for construction of small office and industrial properties. In Providence, leasing conditions are unchanged and investor demand for commercial properties remains very cautious, even for properties in prime locations. In Portland, downtown and, especially, suburban office markets are seeing positive absorption, with resulting vacancy rates in the single digits in both submarkets.

The outlook is mostly optimistic across the District, although Hartford and Providence contacts expect slower improvement in commercial real estate fundamentals than do contacts in Boston and Portland. Respondents note a couple of downside risks to commercial real estate investment, including recent property tax increases in Boston and, for some, costs of compliance with the Dodd-Frank Act.

Residential Real Estate

December saw a strong end to 2014, with closed sales of single family homes increasing in all six New England states compared with December 2013. Condominium sales also increased in every state except Massachusetts. The median sales price for single family homes continued to rise in every state except Connecticut (where prices decreased), while condominium prices rose in Massachusetts and Vermont but declined in Rhode Island, New Hampshire and Connecticut. Contacts in Connecticut and Rhode Island emphasized that while Realtors are feeling very positive, the housing market will not be fully "normal" until shadow inventory and distressed sales are reduced further. In other states, lack of inventory remains a concern. In Massachusetts, for example, December was only the second month of the past six with a year-over-year increase in home sales, while prices have increased 26 out of the last 27 months. Contacts in Massachusetts believe these patterns are driven primarily by a shortage of inventory. The level of inventory heading into January in Massachusetts is the lowest in a decade, with only 3.7 months of supply for single family homes and 2.3 months of supply in the condominium market (Realtors say the market is balanced when a 6- to 7-month supply is available).

First District contacts express concern about the possible lasting impact of the unusually harsh recent weather. In Massachusetts and Connecticut, where January data are available, pending and closed sales were down. Contacts across New England report that demand, despite the weather, remains strong but that new listings and hence inventory will decline as homeowners continue to dig themselves out. As one contact in Massachusetts says "the weather will likely only exacerbate the supply-and-demand imbalance in our market and put upward pressure on prices," Longer term, Realtors remain optimistic about the coming year and are hopeful that interest rates will remain low to help potential buyers.

SECOND DISTRICT—NEW YORK

Growth in the Second District's economy has continued to expand at a moderate pace since the last report. Businesses report that, while selling prices remain mostly stable, cost pressures have increased, including more widespread indications of rising wages. Labor market conditions, more generally, have shown further signs of strengthening in early 2015. Consumer spending has been a bit stronger, on balance, since the last report: both general merchandise retailers and auto dealers note improved sales, despite relatively harsh winter weather. Tourism activity has remained robust in recent weeks, and consumer confidence climbed to another multi-year high. Housing markets were steady to stronger in early 2015. Office markets have been mixed but mostly steady since year end, while the market for industrial space has continued to strengthen. Commercial and multi-family residential construction have picked up somewhat, but new single-family construction has been hindered by bad weather. Finally, banks report steady to stronger loan demand, further narrowing in loan spreads, and steady to lower delinquency rates.

Consumer Spending

Retail sales have improved somewhat, on balance, since the last report. A major general merchandise chain indicates that sales were up strongly from a year ago and also above plan in January but slowed a bit and were on plan in the first half of February. Similarly, a major retail contact in upstate New York describes January as a solid month and February as fairly strong. In both cases, harsh winter weather was said to have hindered business somewhat. In general, retailers report that inventories are in good shape and that discounting remains prevalent.

Reports from auto dealers point to a pickup in vehicle sales. Dealers in both the Rochester and Buffalo areas report that new vehicle sales strengthened in January and remained fairly brisk in early February, despite harsh winter weather. Contacts also note continued improvement in the used car market. An early-February auto show in Buffalo was reportedly well attended, despite the weather. Auto dealers note that both wholesale and retail credit conditions remain in good shape.

Consumer confidence in the region improved further in January, rising to a more than 7-year high in both New York State and the broader Middle Atlantic region (NY, NJ, PA). Tourism activity has remained strong in early 2015. Hotel occupancy rates have been running slightly ahead of a year earlier in the Buffalo and Albany areas. By contrast, both hotel occupancy and revenues were down from a year ago in New York City, when business had been boosted by the Super Bowl. Broadway theaters report that year-to-date attendance and revenues were up more than 15 percent from 2014 levels.

Construction and Real Estate

The District's housing markets have strengthened somewhat in early 2015. New York City's residential rental market has firmed slightly: rents in Manhattan and Brooklyn are reported to be up moderately from a year ago, while they have been steady at an elevated levels in Queens. The inventory of available rentals has risen at the high end of the market—especially in Brooklyn— reflecting new development, but remains fairly tight overall. Rents across the rest of the District are up roughly 2 percent over the past year.

New York City's co-op and condo market has been fairly brisk thus far in 2015, despite harsh weather: sales volume was down moderately from the unusually high levels of a year ago, but still high, while selling prices were up moderately and have roughly recovered to pre-recession peak levels. Housing markets across the rest of New York State and New Jersey have mostly been sluggish, in part due to the inclement weather, though Buffalo area Realtors note solid market conditions in January and early February, despite the weather.

Looking at commercial real estate across the District, office markets have been generally stable, while industrial markets have continued to strengthen. Manhattan's office availability rate rose nearly a full percentage point since year end, mainly reflecting new projects coming on line, while rents continued to climb and were up 4 percent from early-2014 levels. Elsewhere across the District, however, office availability rates were little changed— at a fairly low level of 11 percent in Long Island and just under 13 percent across upstate New York, but at an elevated level of near 18 percent in northern New Jersey and Westchester-Fairfield counties. Industrial availability rates continue to edge down across the District and are at or near multi-year lows in Long Island, as well as Westchester and Fairfield counties.

Commercial construction has remained fairly listless overall, though office construction has picked up in Manhattan and northern New Jersey while industrial construction has picked up somewhat across upstate New York. Multi-family residential construction has been fairly strong across much of the District, though single-family construction has been hindered by weather.

Other Business Activity

Contacts in leisure, hospitality, business services, transportation, and wholesale trade report that activity has picked up in early 2015; businesses in education and health and finance report stable activity; while information industry contacts note some weakening. Manufacturing firms report that activity continued to expand at a modest pace in early 2015; while they have grown less optimistic about the near-term outlook, on balance, a growing proportion plan to increase capital spending in the months ahead. Both manufacturing and service firms report stable selling prices, though service sector firms note increasing pressure on input prices.

The labor market has continued to strengthen since the last report, with some reports of increased wage pressures. One major New York City employment agency maintains that the job market has tightened considerably in recent months and that it is stronger, across the board, than it has been in eight years. This contact also notes that wages have accelerated, especially for workers with any computer skills. More broadly, business contacts report that they continue to increase employment, on balance, and considerably more firms plan to add than cut jobs in the months ahead. Service-sector firms also indicate increasingly widespread wage hikes.

Financial Developments

Small- to medium-sized banks across the District report increased demand for residential mortgage loans, commercial mortgages, and commercial and industrial loans, but a slight pullback in demand for consumer loans and for refinancing. Credit standards were reported to be unchanged across all loan categories. Bankers report a decrease in spreads of loan rates over cost of funds across all loan categories—particularly in commercial mortgages, where nearly half of those surveyed note lower spreads and none report higher spreads. Respondents also reported no change in the average deposit rate. Finally, banking contacts again report lower delinquency rates on consumer loans but little change in delinquencies in other categories.

THIRD DISTRICT — PHILADELPHIA

Aggregate business activity in the Third District continued to grow at a modest pace during this current Beige Book period. Most of the observed differences in growth stem from year-over-year comparisons with the early 2014 months that were battered by severe winter weather. This was especially true for tourism, new home construction, and existing home sales; all three sectors benefited from a somewhat milder winter this year. In contrast, manufacturers reported only slight growth after a somewhat faster pace during the previous period. Auto dealers, staffing firms, and other general service-sector firms continued to report a moderate pace of growth, as did transportation services. Nonauto retailers continued to report modest growth, while tourism appeared to have regained a strong level of activity similar to last year as snow settled on ski resorts. Residential builders responded with mixed reports that offered some optimism for a better 2015. Overall, brokers noted some slight improvement in activity. The commercial real estate sectors continued to report modest growth for construction and for leasing of existing commercial properties.

Lending volumes continued to grow at a modest pace, and credit quality continued to improve; however, increasing numbers of contacts expressed concern about weak underwriting standards. As in the previous Beige Book, contacts reported slight increases in wages, home prices, and general price levels. Contacts continued to anticipate moderate growth of economic activity over the next six months.

Manufacturing. Third District manufacturers reported that current activity continued to grow during the latest Beige Book period but only at a slight pace. Nearly as many firms indicated declines in activity as increases. New orders and shipments also grew more slowly; the percentage of firms reporting decreases in new orders and shipments rose further compared with the last period. Gains in activity appeared to be stronger among makers of industrial machinery, electronic equipment, and paper products; activity appeared weaker among makers of primary and fabricated metal products. Overall, most firms reported that declining energy prices were having a positive impact on their own production costs and on potential demand via consumer channels; however, some firms reported weaker demand or a weaker outlook for demand from customers serving energy production sectors.

Expectations of growth during the next six months remained positive but slipped from historically high levels to levels that are more typical of an expansionary period. The percentage of firms anticipating positive growth dropped to less than 50 percent for the first time in more than a year. Despite that shift, firms reported little change in expectations of future employment and capital expenditures, with about one-third anticipating increases and about one-tenth anticipating decreases.

Retail. Third District contacts have continued to report modest growth in nonauto retail sales since the prior Beige Book period. An operator of area malls reported that sales growth finished solidly for the holiday season and that their retailers were indicating good activity through January and into February. Restaurants experienced a renewed growth of customers during the fourth quarter of 2014 and attributed part of the demand as a reaction to falling gasoline prices. "Consumers had a great month" during the holiday season, according to an outlet mall operator, further bolstering reports that stores moved the most goods via heavy promotions. Contacts remain cautiously optimistic for 2015; however, margins remain tight for retailers, and most shoppers remain focused on low prices.

Auto dealers continued to report moderate growth in sales year over year. A Pennsylvania contact described sales levels throughout the state as being strong overall through mid-February despite the typically softer seasonal levels. New Jersey contacts reported strong statewide sales for January; however, weather was taking a toll on early February sales. Auto dealers expect growth to continue in 2015 as it had in 2014.

Finance. Third District financial firms continued to report modest increases in total loan volume since the previous Beige Book. Volumes decreased seasonally for credit card lines as consumers pay down for several weeks following their holiday spending. Strong growth was reported for other consumer credit lines, including auto loans, and for commercial real estate loans. Moderate growth was reported for commercial and industrial lending, while modest growth was reported for home mortgages. Only slight growth was reported for home equity lines of credit. Increasing numbers of contacts expressed concerns that competition has lowered lending standards, undercut margins, and is beginning to lower overall credit quality. Many indicated that they saw no signs of inflationary pressures. Banking contacts tended to be most positive about economic prospects in central Pennsylvania, the Lehigh Valley area, and the Philadelphia market. Nearly all contacts have grown more optimistic about growth prospects for 2015.

Real Estate and Construction. Third District homebuilders provided mixed reports. A New Jersey builder was encouraged by good levels of new contract signings in January and February on the heels of a strong end-of-year close. One central Pennsylvania builder was close to budget in January but reported a slowdown in February. Generally, builders reported that housing starts have slowed with the cold and snow. Also, builders reported that regular price increases of construction materials leaves little room within their own tight margins for addressing wage pressures from their subcontractors. Builders anticipate a better year in 2015. Brokers reported that existing home sales were greater in December and January on a year-over-year basis; sales growth was the greatest in central Pennsylvania, while sales were essentially unchanged along the Jersey shore. Contacts noted that the positive comparisons are made with a 2013 sales season pounded by winter storms. Contacts continued to report slight overall increases in home prices, except in the city of Philadelphia where sales and prices are rising faster. Brokers are generally more optimistic for a return to growth in 2015.

Construction and leasing continued at a modest pace, according to nonresidential real estate contacts. New construction continued to be dominated by industrial/warehouse projects, urban apartment dwellings, and public infrastructure, including sand reclamation projects along the Jersey shore. Contacts reported that continuing incremental improvements in leasing activity in downtown and suburban Philadelphia is leading to some upward push on rents, especially for Class A or better office space. Center City residential and retail markets also continued to be active, as well as several select suburban office markets. Contacts remained optimistic for the ongoing growth of both new construction and leasing activity in 2015.

Services. Third District service-sector firms have continued to report moderate growth in activity since the previous Beige Book. About half of all firms reported increases in new orders and sales. A transportation services analyst reported that the absolute volume of traffic was approaching levels last attained during the prior expansion, which means greater highway congestion. The record volume has occurred even as trucking capacity was freeing up due to recent investments in new trucks, new drivers, and a temporary lull from regulatory constraints. The analyst also roughly estimated that the lower diesel fuel costs generated a 1 percent savings on the cost of goods shipped. Staffing contacts throughout the Third District reported positive employment trends across a broad spectrum of economic sectors. Companies reportedly kept busy at year-end with less of the typical slump in the demand for temps. Firms reported that direct hires have picked up, that the majority of hires are due to economic growth rather than replacement, and that temp placements are stronger still when compared with last year, when winter storms closed businesses for several days at a time. Staffing firms remained very positive for growth prospects in 2015. Staffing contacts described tight margins and little change in wage pressures. Among all service-sector contacts, more than three-fourths reported expectations that growth trends for their firms will remain positive over the next six months; none anticipated declines.

Third District tourist areas reported improving conditions as the winter has worn on. Despite early season snow, the ski season had a slow start. However, contacts report that activity is now about even with last year, which was a very good season. Contacts remain concerned about the long-term impacts of the Atlantic City casino closings on the local economy and especially on the city's fiscal health. Surprisingly, casino revenues posted a rare positive year-over-year increase in January; however, it was mostly due to very weak numbers during the severe winter weather last year.

Prices and Wages. Overall, Third District contacts reported little change to the steady, slight pace of price level increases that was seen in other recent Beige Book periods. Manufacturing contacts reported little change in the prices they pay and the prices received for their products since the prior period. The percentage of firms reporting increases fell nearly to the same percentage of firms reporting decreases. Among nonmanufacturing firms, a somewhat lower percentage of contacts reported increases of prices paid and prices received since the prior period, and a slightly greater percentage have reported decreases; overall price pressures have lessened. Manufacturers and construction firms continued to note wage pressures to attract skilled workers. Other contacts, including those from staffing firms, continued to note little significant change in wage pressures.

FOURTH DISTRICT – CLEVELAND

On balance, the Fourth District's economy expanded at a modest pace during the past six weeks. Activity at manufacturing plants was mixed. In residential real estate markets, single-family home prices rose, while unit volumes were fairly stable; nonresidential construction markets strengthened. Retailers and auto dealers reported that post-holiday sales were slightly above year-ago levels. Shale gas activity contracted due to low oil and natural gas prices. Freight shipments remained strong, but capacity issues are limiting growth. The demand for business and consumer credit slowly moved higher.

Payrolls were little changed on net, except in manufacturing, where demand for production and sales personnel increased. Staffing firms reported that job openings and placements in financial services, healthcare, and manufacturing had risen slightly. Upward pressure on wages is limited to experienced and technically skilled personnel across industry sectors. Overall, input and finished goods prices were steady. We heard reports about declines in steel prices, diesel fuel surcharges, and rising prices for some building materials.

Manufacturing. Factory contacts reported mixed activity during the past six weeks. Apart from seasonal factors affecting demand, declining orders were attributed to lower oil prices, a strengthening dollar, and weakening economic conditions in Europe. Growth in the motor vehicle and construction industries boosted new orders for some contacts. Overall, year-to-date results were generally better compared to those in 2014. Looking forward, manufacturers are fairly bullish about business activity. Factors tempering growth expectations include exposure to foreign markets and the price of oil. Steel producers cited declining prices, a strong dollar, aggressive imports, and a decline in oil and gas drilling as factors contributing to shipments that were softer than expected. Autos are still seen as a strong end market and orders from construction contractors improved. Several of our steel contacts downgraded their 2015 forecasts and cut inventory. Auto production at District assembly plants continued at a robust pace. Total production in 2014 was 4.5 percent higher compared to the previous year.

Capital spending during the past six weeks was mainly for new equipment, including IT, and plant expansion. Several manufacturers noted that they have boosted capital budgets since the beginning of the year primarily because of business acquisitions. A majority of our contacts reported lower raw material prices, especially for petroleum-based products and steel. Several contacts attributed falling prices to lower global demand for commodity metals. Finished goods prices held steady. There was a notable pickup in hiring, especially for production and sales personnel. Wage pressures are limited to engineering and computer-system employees.

Real Estate and Construction. Sales of new and existing single-family homes for all of 2014 were slightly below levels seen in the prior year, while the average sales price was 4 percent higher. Home builders were evenly split in their assessment of market conditions since the start of the year. Softening was attributed to cold weather and a shortage of desirable lots against a backdrop of stringent mortgage standards. New-home contracts were mainly in the move-up price-point categories. The first-time buyer market remains weak. There was a large drop in the number of single-family construction starts since our last report. Nonetheless, as the spring season approaches, homebuilders are fairly optimistic in their outlook. They believe the potential for higher interest rates might serve as an impetus for potential buyers to sign a purchase contract. Most builders have not raised prices since the beginning of the year.

Nonresidential builders reported pre-construction activity generally ranging from moderate to robust, and they indicated that the level of activity has increased relative to a year ago. Customers are more confident in the sustainability of the economy, and they are now ready to move forward on projects that had been postponed. Market demand is broad based, although demand for multi-unit housing and industrial and office space is strongest. Builders are adding to their backlog on a steady basis, and their backlogs are larger than a year ago. Several contacts noted that they are becoming more selective when bidding projects, and they expect margins to widen as the year progresses. Capital spending by general contractors was mainly for replacement of heavy machinery and technology.

Materials prices were stable apart from increases for drywall and concrete. Builders are expecting overall increases of about 3 percent this year. Diesel fuel surcharges were reduced, but lower oil prices have not passed through to other petroleum-based products. Payrolls were flat on net due to the winter weather. As spring approaches, general contractors expect a period of fairly robust hiring, including craft workers, project engineers, and managers. Little wage pressure was reported, and it was limited to experienced craft workers. Subcontractors are pushing through rate increases at a faster pace than general contractors had anticipated; these increases are to cover rising costs, including for labor, and to widen margins.

Consumer Spending. Retailers were generally satisfied with post-holiday sales, and they reported that January revenues were slightly higher than those in January 2014. Product lines in highest demand included cold-weather apparel, electronics, and health and wellness. Most contacts expect second-quarter sales to be somewhat higher year-over-year, as lower gasoline prices begin having a greater impact on consumer spending. The increase in promotions that began early in the fourth quarter has been scaled back, which contributed to slightly higher margins. Vendor and shelf prices were steady, other than for declines in dairy products and apparel. Beef prices remain at historic highs. Several contacts reported reductions in planned capital spending for fiscal year 2015. Spending since the beginning of the year was concentrated in real estate and e-commerce. Hiring is limited to new store openings.

New motor vehicles sales during January were slightly higher than those of a year ago and in December. The share of SUV and truck sales increased by about 7 percentage points compared to last January, which some dealers attributed to significantly lower gasoline prices. Looking at 2015, dealers anticipate that the year-over-year change in unit volume will be positive, but increases will not be as strong as in 2014. New inventory is in line with sales. Used vehicle sales are up slightly over last January. Capital spending this year by dealerships is mainly for maintenance and facility upgrades. Little change in payrolls is expected during the winter months. Dealer service departments are feeling wage pressures because of a lack of qualified technicians and mechanics.

Banking. Bankers reported that demand for business credit showed moderate growth during the past six weeks. While demand was described as broad based, it was strongest for commercial real estate, and commercial and industrial loans. Consumer credit demand moved slightly higher, primarily for home equity products. Auto lending has softened. Interest rates were steady to down slightly for business and consumer credit. Many of our contacts noted an improvement in their residential mortgage business, more so on the refinancing side, which they attributed to a decline in interest rates. Delinquency rates held steady, at very low levels, and bankers expect little change going forward. No changes were made to loan-application standards. Core deposits remain strong. Payrolls were little changed on net. Hiring was mainly for jobs in commercial lending, computer-related services, and regulatory compliance. Wage pressure was felt in each of these job categories.

Energy. Little change in District coal production was reported. Spot prices for metallurgical and steam coal declined since our last report. Activity in the Marcellus and Utica shales contracted due to low oil and natural gas prices. The number of drilling rigs in the District shrank 19 percent since mid-December. Reports indicated that oil and gas producers have made significant cuts to planned capital spending for 2015, though midstream companies involved in the build out of the oil and gas infrastructure have not yet shown an inclination to pull back investment in existing projects. One energy executive said that while oil inventories are high at this time, with a cutback in production, oil stocks should decline at a rapid pace. These events could serve as the impetus for a strengthening of oil prices sometime later in 2015. Overall pricing for materials and equipment was flat. Some layoffs in the oil and gas sector and their supplier industries were reported.

Freight Transportation. On balance, little change was seen in freight volume since our last report, with many carriers operating at a high level. Volume growth was seen in construction materials, crude oil, and natural gas liquids. Any softening was attributed to seasonal factors. Our contacts expect that the economy will continue to expand this year; however, capacity constraints may limit top line growth. Little change in pricing was noted other than lower revenue from fuel surcharges. Capital spending in 2015 is projected to be strong. Some carriers reported increasing existing budgets. Monies are largely allocated for replacing aging equipment. Capacity expansion is limited by driver availability. Difficulty in attracting and retaining drivers and maintenance technicians is putting upward pressure on wages for both job categories. A majority of our contacts cited a significant rise in health insurance premiums at the start of the year.

FIFTH DISTRICT–RICHMOND

Overview. On balance, the Fifth District economy grew at a slower pace since the previous Beige Book. District manufacturing activity weakened, with shipments and new orders flattening. Retail sales growth slowed. Revenues in the non-retail service sector grew more rapidly, and tourism was at normal seasonal levels. In finance, both consumer and commercial lending increased since the previous report. Residential real estate activity expanded moderately; activity in commercial real estate markets increased at a modest pace. Agribusinesses experienced seasonal slowing. Coal production was unchanged. Production of natural gas was also unchanged, although levels were above those of a year ago. Natural gas prices declined in recent weeks. Demand for labor generally rose.

According to our most recent surveys, manufacturing employment grew modestly and average wages in the sector increased more quickly since the previous Beige Book. In the service sector, hiring was little changed and average wages rose more rapidly. Service sector prices and manufacturers' prices paid and prices received climbed more slowly in recent weeks.

Manufacturing. District manufacturing growth stalled since the previous report, with shipments and new orders flattening since the start of the year. Inventories of raw materials and finished goods rose moderately, but more slowly than in the previous report. A producer of dental equipment commented that lower patient counts had resulted in reduced sales of his products per doctor. Also, a manufacturer of sealing devices said that his company was seeing a general drop in sales. A producer of packaging materials reported a slight decline in production at his plant, and an auto parts manufacturer reported slower revenue growth. In contrast, product demand had risen for a producer of heavy equipment parts, and business was good for a food processor. Manufacturers were upbeat about business prospects for the months ahead. An executive at an electrical instruments firm in Virginia said that shipments and new orders were unchanged, but that his company had recently increased capital spending. A North Carolina textile manufacturer reported plans to increase capacity this year. An executive whose firm fabricates heavy construction products used for infrastructure said shipments were up recently. He stated that the company had increased capital spending over the past year and that he was expecting solid business growth again this year. A wood products manufacturer also reported stronger sales. Manufacturers' prices paid and prices received rose at a slower pace in recent weeks, according to contacts.

Ports. District port activity remained strong since the previous Beige Book. Port officials continued to report high volumes of container traffic, particularly for grain exports and imports of retail products. Exports of petroleum products rose sharply at one port. Auto imports softened slightly since our last report, but imports of "roll-on/roll-off" equipment rose. Dockworker contract issues at West Coast ports have resulted in increased inquiries and some ship diversions to East Coast ports.

Retail. Retail activity slowed in the weeks since our previous report. Sales of cars and light trucks were generally flat, according to dealers in Virginia, North Carolina, and South Carolina. A dealer in the eastern panhandle of West Virginia reported slightly slower sales. Grocery and convenience stores reported a decline in food sales in in the past month. According to the manager at a Virginia chain of discount stores, holiday and post-holiday sales were softer than expected, but still higher than a year ago. Several small retailers in the Richmond area also reported good year-over-year growth in revenues. Retail price inflation slowed since our last report. A wholesaler of residential building materials reported supply price increases, which he expects to be able to pass through to his customers.

Services. Revenues at non-retail service firms strengthened since the previous Beige Book. Executives at telecommunications, accounting, and travel firms reported faster revenue growth in recent weeks. In addition, District hospital executives reported an uptick in demand, partly from flu outbreaks. Services prices rose at a slower pace since our previous report.

Tourism was generally at normal seasonal levels in recent weeks, with most contacts indicating a typical slowdown in activity for this time of year. However, a Charleston, South Carolina contact reported strong tourist activity. A contact on the outer banks of North Carolina said the weekend of Presidents' Day and Valentine's Day brought solid hotel bookings and rentals, with tourists attracted by off-season specials and several planned events for visitors. Hotel managers are expecting a greater-than-seasonal pick-up in the months ahead. A Maryland hotelier reported an increase in group and conference bookings for the six months ahead, and a Virginia hotel manager expects summer business to be very strong. A resort manager in West Virginia reported strong growth in current bookings and in sales of passes for the remainder of this season and next winter. Hotels and resorts reported no change in rates.

Finance. Loan demand increased slightly since the previous Beige Book. Residential mortgage demand rose in Virginia and West Virginia, especially for refinancing. According to a Virginia banker, consumer lending increased as customers financed home improvement projects, cars, and luxury goods like boats. Commercial and industrial lending increased in Maryland, South Carolina, and Richmond, Virginia. In West Virginia, a banker reported that commercial lending rose in some sectors but was not robust overall. Two community bankers, one in North Carolina and one in Virginia, said that commercial loan demand softened in recent weeks. Deposits increased, according to bankers in North Carolina, Virginia, and West Virginia. Throughout the District, mortgage interest rates were reported to be slightly lower. Several contacts also reported relaxed credit standards. An executive in Maryland said that large banks were easing underwriting standards, and a Virginia banker noted that increased competition has led to some lowering of underwriting standards among community banks as well. A number of contacts throughout the District said credit quality was unchanged, despite an apparent easing in standards.

Real Estate. Residential real estate activity increased moderately in recent weeks. Realtors in Virginia and North Carolina reported increased sales, especially for higher end homes in North Carolina.

Buyer traffic picked up in several locations, which a Virginia Realtor attributed to lower interest rates. In contrast, a West Virginia contact said first-time home buyers are hesitant because closing costs and fees have gone up. Average days on the market varied by location and sales prices were generally reported as flat to rising slightly. Inventories decreased in Washington, D.C., Northern Virginia, and Charlotte, North Carolina. In Northern Virginia, custom home builders were looking for building lots. A North Carolina Realtor said that land availability was an issue.

Since our last Beige Book, activity in commercial real estate markets increased at a modest pace. Realtors in Maryland, North Carolina, South Carolina, and Virginia reported a moderate increase in retail leasing, especially for smaller spaces and grocery stores. Office space leasing was unchanged according to contacts in North Carolina and Virginia. However office leasing picked up Charleston, West Virginia, and a real estate contact in the Wilmington, North Carolina area said that class A and class B office space was being absorbed at a faster pace. He also said that the market for industrial space had improved. A South Carolina Realtor reported that the office sector slowed slightly in Charleston due to lack of available space and the industrial market is growing even though much of the inventory is functionally obsolete. Office and industrial vacancy rates declined in other areas of South Carolina, but were unchanged elsewhere. Several contacts throughout the District reported new construction projects, especially for supermarkets, groceries and grocery-anchored shopping centers, medical centers, and apartment buildings.

Agriculture and Natural Resources. Since our previous Beige Book, agribusiness contacts reported typical seasonal slowdowns, but business conditions were slightly stronger than at this time last year. Additionally, a farmer in Virginia said that the spring outlook was "really good." Contacts in South Carolina and Virginia reported planting and harvesting of sod, shrubs, and trees, although adverse weather conditions reduced the number of days available to do so. Input prices were reported as mostly stable in recent weeks, while sod prices rose slightly. A farmer in South Carolina expressed concern over low commodity prices and difficulty navigating recent insurance legislation.

Coal production was unchanged overall since our previous report. In central West Virginia, production decreased marginally year over year; however, production rose slightly in the northern part of the state. Coal prices declined since the prior Beige Book. Production of natural gas was unchanged, but levels were above those of a year ago. Natural gas prices continued to decline modestly in recent weeks.

Labor Markets. Reports on labor demand were mostly positive since our previous Beige Book. Contacts across the District reported the recent hiring of engineers, salespeople, production workers, marketers, and retail workers. Demand for employees rose in construction, hospitality, manufacturing, IT, grocery, transportation, and management. An executive said that demand had recently increased for part-time workers but was basically flat for full time employees. Throughout the District, several industries reported continued difficulty finding both unskilled and skilled labor. An office staffing executive in

Charleston, South Carolina remarked that a shortage of quality candidates was leading to multiple job offers and some upward wage pressure. Similarly, the shortage of truck drivers was pushing up wages, according to one report. According to our most recent surveys, manufacturing employment growth has been modest and average wages in the sector have risen more quickly since the previous Beige Book. In the service sector, hiring was little changed, although average wages rose more rapidly.

SIXTH DISTRICT – ATLANTA

The Sixth District's economy continued to grow at a moderate pace from January to early February. The majority of contacts are optimistic and expect near-term growth to be sustained at, or slightly above, current rates.

Overall, District retail reports were positive over the reporting period. Motor vehicle dealer contacts indicated lower gas prices helped spur an increase in light truck sales. The District's tourism industry remained a bright spot with reports of increased activity in the business and convention segments. Residential real estate reports on home sales were mixed; however, both brokers and builders continued to witness modest home price appreciation. Commercial real estate markets continued to see improvements in demand and nonresidential construction was ahead of year-ago levels. Manufacturers reported increases in new orders and production. Bankers indicated that loan demand was strong for most business lines. On balance, the District's labor force continued to grow. Firms continued to cite nominal wage increases for most jobs and other input costs remained subdued.

Consumer Spending and Tourism. After experiencing a moderate 2014 holiday season, District merchants appeared optimistic during the early months of 2015. Recreation-and-vacation-centric retailers experienced solid overall growth last year, and expect a similar trend for the first half of 2015. Casual dining establishments saw an uptick in volume as consumers seem to be trading up from fast food options. Many contacts cited evidence, such as a noticeable increase in purchases of light trucks that lower gasoline prices had led to increased spending on other goods and services.

Hospitality contacts reported an increase in business and convention bookings. Reports from industry contacts also indicated that the U.S. dollar exchange rate was not negatively affecting international visitors to the District. Lower gas prices were also reported as a contributing factor to a rise in visitors of drive-to destinations. Hoteliers anticipate that the next three to six months will outperform last year based on advanced bookings.

Real Estate and Construction. Since the last report, District brokers' reports on home sales activity improved a bit. Most contacts reported that home sales were flat to up slightly compared with the year earlier level. Brokers continued to report modest home price appreciation. The majority of brokers indicated that inventory levels either remained flat or had fallen from the prior year's level and noted that buyer traffic was flat to slightly up compared with a year ago. Brokers noted that they expect home sales activity to increase over the next three months.

Incoming signals from District builders have dampened a bit since the last report. Builders characterized construction activity and new home sales activity as flat to down slightly from the year earlier level. Many builders indicated that their inventory of unsold homes was flat to slightly up from a year ago, and noted that buyer traffic was flat to slightly down compared with the year-ago level. However, most builders continued to report some degree of home price appreciation. The outlook among builders for new home sales and construction activity over the next three months was fairly positive, with most indicating that they expect activity to increase modestly.

Commercial real estate brokers around the District continued to report improving demand, though they cautioned that the rate of improvement varied by metropolitan area, submarket, and property type. Commercial contractors indicated that nonresidential construction activity had increased from the year-ago level across the District and noted the strength in apartment construction has persisted. Most contacts reported a backlog that was greater than their year earlier level. The outlook among District commercial real estate contacts remained positive.

Manufacturing and Transportation. District contacts indicated that manufacturing activity rebounded during the current reporting period, following a modest slowdown in December. Increases in new orders and production were notable, and factory employment continued to increase. Supplier delivery times slowed slightly, while contacts reported a moderate rise in finished inventory levels. With over half of contacts expecting production levels to increase over the next three to six months, optimism remained consistent with the previous reporting period.

Transportation contacts reported an expansion of activity from January to early February. Trucking companies cited steady freight volume and notable year-over-year increases in tonnage. District ports reported significant increases in bulk cargo, container traffic, and shipments of autos from year-earlier levels. Contacts in the air cargo industry reported record freight tonnage led by strong international activity. Railroads cited marked year-over-year increases in the shipment of metallic ores, petroleum products, grain and aggregates, but volume declines in phosphates and iron and steel scrap metals. However, contacts did note that west coast port congestion may be contributing to some of the District's port activity, particularly where increases were noted. Substantial, ongoing capital investments in rail infrastructure continued to be reported.

Banking and Finance. Credit conditions were largely unchanged from the previous reporting period. Overall, credit remained readily available and small businesses reported more access to credit. Loan demand was strong among most lines of business, particularly commercial and mortgage lending. Bankers noted increased lending to businesses such as hotels and restaurants. Loan pricing and structure remained competitive. Banking contacts indicated their lending standards remained fairly conservative.

Employment and Prices. Overall, businesses indicated that they continued to add to payrolls. However, contacts continued to report difficulty filling skilled positions in the information technology, finance, construction, and manufacturing industries. In addition, a number of contacts noted that retail and other service-based entry-level positions were becoming more difficult to fill. Some firms engaged in energy exploration and production and oilfield service providers reported layoffs resulting from declines in energy prices.

Input cost pressures remained subdued for most firms. The Atlanta Fed's poll of business contacts in January indicated that, on average, firms anticipate unit costs to rise 1.7 percent over the coming 12 months, down two-tenths of a percentage point from the December reading. The decline in fuel prices was overwhelmingly seen as an opportunity to improve margins rather than lower prices. Plans for wage increases in 2015 were little changed, with most contacts budgeting two-to-three percent increases for the year. However, figures remained higher for more competitive or difficult-to-fill positions, and several contacts indicated increasing entry-level wages.

Natural Resources and Agriculture. Crude oil storage continued to expand onshore and off, which contributed to high crude oil inventory levels across the Gulf Coast. Impacts of declining energy prices have been mixed. Petrochemical, industrial power, transportation, and manufacturing contacts with business dealings in the energy sector described positive outcomes, such as improved profit margins from lower fuel and feedstock costs, as well as steady project bookings through 2015. However, firms engaged in exploration and production and oilfield service providers began to report negative effects to business activity, including employee layoffs.

Drought conditions improved in parts of the District although there were still some areas reportedly affected by dry conditions. Florida citrus crop producers continued field practices to combat citrus greening while the USDA announced additional funding to help fight the disease. The most recent 2015 domestic production forecasts for rice, soybeans, peanuts, and cotton were unchanged from a month ago while beef, pork, and broilers production projections were up from the prior month.

SEVENTH DISTRICT—CHICAGO

Summary. Growth in economic activity in the Seventh District remained moderate in January and early February, and contacts expected growth to continue at a similar pace over the next six to twelve months. Consumer spending and manufacturing production rose moderately, while business spending and construction and real estate activity increased modestly. Credit conditions improved on balance. Cost pressures were little changed, and price increases remained limited. Prices of most agricultural commodities declined.

Consumer spending. Growth in consumer spending remained moderate in January and early February. Contacts reported that lower energy prices had a positive effect on retail sales, though not as much as they were hoping. Growth was robust for the general merchandise, clothing, and specialty gift sectors, but slower for food, beverages, furniture, and appliances. The pace of new light vehicle sales held steady, while sales of used vehicles increased. Auto dealers indicated that incentives were not as generous as during the previous reporting period, leading to less floor traffic. Dealers also noted that lower gasoline prices continued to shift the sales mix from cars to light trucks and SUVs.

Business spending. Growth in business spending slowed to a modest pace in January and early February. Most manufacturers and retailers reported comfortable inventory levels. However, transportation disruptions at west coast ports related to the longshoremen labor contract negotiations delayed delivery of some retail items and led some manufacturers to hold higher levels of inventories as a precaution. In addition, some auto dealers reported that inventories were slightly elevated because of over-ordering in December. The pace of current capital spending slowed somewhat, though spending plans for the next six to twelve months continued to indicate steady growth. Outlays were again primarily for replacing industrial and IT equipment, though many contacts also reported spending for capacity expansion. The pace of hiring slowed, but contacts expect continued moderate employment growth in the next six to twelve months. A staffing firm reported demand was holding steady but that job placements were down because it had become increasing difficult to find workers to fill their customers' orders. Contacts again reported strong demand for skilled workers, particularly for those in professional and technical occupations and skilled manufacturing and building trades.

Construction and real estate. Construction and real estate activity increased modestly over the reporting period. Demand for residential construction was mostly unchanged, but with some additional growth in single-family building in urban markets. Home prices and residential rents both increased, while home sales held steady. Solid income growth and expanding credit availability for first-time homebuyers has led real estate contacts to revise up their sales forecasts for 2015. In addition, several contacts observed that markets in low-income areas are finally showing signs of improvement. Nonresidential construction grew moderately, driven primarily by demand for industrial buildings. Commercial real estate activity expanded broadly – vacancies declined, rents rose, and leasing of industrial buildings, office space, and retail space all increased.

Manufacturing. Manufacturing production continued to grow at a moderate pace in January and early February. Activity in the auto industry remained a source of strength for the District, with contacts citing the improving labor market and low gasoline prices as bolstering demand. Auto industry contacts expressed concern, however, that high capacity utilization rates are raising costs through the increased use of overtime and limited time for preventative maintenance. Demand for steel grew steadily. Weak demand abroad combined with the relative strength of the US economy continued to draw in imported steel and push down prices. Most specialty metals manufacturers reported steady gains in new orders and solid order books, though contacts supplying the oil and gas industry reported slowing demand. Contacts also noted that the strong dollar was hurting exports. Sales of heavy machinery and heavy trucks both picked up, and manufacturers of building materials expect steady growth in shipments for 2015.

Banking/finance. Credit conditions improved on balance over the reporting period. Equity markets moved higher and volatility declined. In contrast, interest rate volatility ticked up. Business loan demand increased, driven by new equipment purchases and expansions of existing facilities. Credit line utilization by middle-market firms increased slightly and business banking contacts generally noted a better than expected start to the year. Consumer loan demand increased across multiple segments. Mortgage refinancings surged and new applications rose in response to lower mortgage rates. Demand for auto loans remained strong and growth in new credit card applications increased. One banking contact noted that downward pressure on auto loan rates was leading to increased competition for sub-prime borrowers.

Prices/costs. Overall, cost pressures were little changed in January and early February. Energy and steel prices decreased, while cement and drywall prices rose. Retail food prices generally declined, with the exception of meat and dairy prices. The transportation delays at west coast ports pushed up shipping costs as some contacts were forced to use alternate, more expensive supply routes. More contacts said they increased prices than during the last reporting period. Of those reporting price increases, most cited increased demand or pricing power as the reason for the increase. Wage and non-wage costs changed little on balanced. Wage pressures continued to be more pronounced for skilled workers than for unskilled workers. However, a staffing firm reported some willingness from its clients to raise pay rates for unskilled workers in order to reduce turnover.

Agriculture. Corn, soybean, and wheat prices were lower than during the previous reporting period, although they recovered some in recent weeks. Apart from fuel costs, input costs for spring planting have remained steady. Some farmers purchased lower quality seeds than last year to reduce their planting costs. Even though higher relative input costs were likely to shift acres toward soybean production and away from corn, there were reports that farmers were reluctant to plan major changes in crop rotations. Contacts also noted plans to return some marginal ground to pasture or hay production, instead of planting corn or soybeans this spring. Hog production was strong, with no major issues from diseases, which had cut production last year. This pushed down pork prices substantially, and consumers began substituting from beef to pork. However, somewhat lower cattle prices did not translate into lower retail prices for beef. Milk prices declined amid rising stocks of dairy products and stalled exports. The slowdowns at ports along the west coast hurt exports of many agricultural products.

EIGHTH DISTRICT — ST. LOUIS

Summary

Economic activity in the Eighth District has increased at a moderate pace since the previous Beige Book. Recent reports of planned activity in manufacturing and services have been positive on net. Reports from retail contacts have also been positive. Overall residential real estate market conditions have improved, while commercial and industrial real estate markets and construction have been mixed. Lending activity during the past three months has increased at a sample of District banks. Over the past three months, compared with the same period a year ago, wages have grown moderately while employment and prices charged to consumers have grown modestly.

Consumer Spending

Retail contacts in the District noted that sales during the first two months of 2015 have stayed the same or increased relative to a year ago. The majority of retail contacts noted that sales were in line with expectations.

Reports from auto dealers were also generally positive. Contacts noted that auto sales during the first two months of 2015 have stayed the same or increased, compared with same period last year. Approximately half of auto dealers contacted reported that, relative to a year earlier, sales shifted toward new vehicles from used vehicles; the other half of contacts were split between no change and more used car sales. Similarly, contacts also noted that more high-end cars have been sold than low-end cars, compared with a year ago.

Manufacturing and Other Business Activity

Reports of plans for manufacturing activity since the previous Beige Book have been positive on net. Producers in the apparel, automobile, aerospace, and chemical manufacturing industries announced plans to hire additional employees and expand operations in the District. In contrast, firms that manufacture electronic equipment and primary metals announced plans to lay-off workers or close facilities. Hiring reports from food manufacturers were mixed. A recent survey of manufacturers indicated that most firms increased employment during the past three months, and average wages per employee also increased for the majority of firms surveyed.

Reports of plans in the District's service sector have been positive since the previous report. Firms that provide business support, air and truck transportation, recreation, and health care and social assistance services reported new hiring and expansion plans in the District. In contrast, firms in publishing services plan to lay-off employees. Firms in educational services reported both layoffs and new hires.

Real Estate and Construction

Home sales increased in the Eighth District on a year-over-year basis. Compared with the same period in 2013, December 2014 monthly home sales were up 5 percent in Louisville, 11 percent in Little Rock, and 29 percent in St. Louis; home sales remained the same in Memphis. December 2014 monthly single-family housing permits increased in the majority of the District metro areas compared with the same period in 2013. Permits increased 26 percent in Louisville, 49 percent in Little Rock, 13 percent in St. Louis, and 17 percent in Memphis.

Commercial and industrial real estate market conditions were mixed throughout most of the District. Contacts in northwest Kentucky reported that a limited supply of commercial real estate is resulting in upward pressure on prices and declining vacancy rates across most property types. Contacts in Memphis reported low industrial vacancy rates. Contacts in Little Rock reported low asking rents in the commercial market. Commercial and industrial construction activity was mixed throughout most of the District. Contacts in northwest Kentucky noted that financing and regulatory constraints are increasing the costs of new commercial construction projects. A contact in Memphis reported improvements in the lending environment for commercial construction projects. Contacts in St. Louis continued to report new large multi-family construction projects in the downtown area. Similarly, contacts in Little Rock noted an increase in multi-family construction projects.

Banking and Finance

A survey of District banks showed that overall lending activity during the past three months increased moderately. For commercial and industrial loans, credit standards continued to be slightly lower, creditworthiness of applicants improved, demand was stronger, and delinquencies were lower. For standard residential mortgage loans, credit standards were mostly unchanged, creditworthiness of applicants improved, demand was somewhat stronger, and delinquencies were slightly lower. For credit cards, standards were unchanged to slightly lower, creditworthiness of applicants was slightly higher, demand was unchanged, and delinquencies were lower. For auto loans and other consumer loans, creditworthiness of applicants was unchanged, demand was unchanged to slightly higher, and delinquencies were lower; credit standards decreased slightly for auto loans and remained unchanged for other consumer loans.

Agriculture and Natural Resources

As of early February, close to 90 percent of the District winter wheat crop was rated in fair or better condition. Total District red meat production during 2014 was largely the same compared with 2013. Missouri exhibited strong production increases in 2014, offsetting decreases observed in other District states. District coal production for January 2015 was about 1.6 percent higher than in January 2014.

Employment, Wages, and Prices

A survey of District businesses indicated that, over the past three months, wages grew moderately while employment and prices charged to consumers grew modestly compared with the same period last year. For employment levels, 56 percent of contacts reported that they have stayed the same compared with the same period last year, 35 percent reported a slight increase, and 9 percent indicated a slight decrease. For prices charged to customers, 56 percent of contacts reported that they have stayed the same compared with the same period last year, 33 percent reported an increase, and 11 percent reported a decrease. Finally, for wages, 51 percent of contacts indicated that they have stayed the same compared with the same period last year, and 46 percent indicated they were higher.

NINTH DISTRICT--MINNEAPOLIS

The Ninth District economy grew at a moderate pace since the previous report. Increased activity was noted in consumer spending, commercial construction, commercial real estate, professional services, and manufacturing. Activity was mixed in tourism and residential real estate and down in residential construction, agriculture, and energy and mining. While labor markets continued to tighten in several areas, signs of loosening were noted in the energy-producing region. Reports of increased wage pressures were noted in some areas. Price pressures were subdued, as oil and gasoline prices decreased during January.

Consumer Spending and Tourism

Consumer spending increased moderately. A North Dakota mall noted that sales were up in January compared with a year ago. A bar and restaurant chain in Minnesota reported strong sales during January compared with last year. Recent light truck and car sales were relatively solid in Montana, according to a representative of an auto dealers association. However, some apparel stores had difficulty selling winter clothing due to relatively mild weather conditions during December and January. As the U.S. dollar strengthened relative to the Canadian dollar over the past few months, border crossings and related retail sales decreased. For example, bridge crossings at the International Bridge in Sault Ste. Marie, Mich., were down 12 percent in December compared with a year earlier.

Tourism conditions were mixed. A lack of snow in many areas of Minnesota slowed snowmobiling and cross-country skiing. Light snowfall and warm weather slowed winter tourism activity in parts of Montana. However, winter tourism activity was solid in the Upper Peninsula of Michigan, where the snowpack was relatively deep. Visits from out-of-state tourists to Montana are expected to increase by 2 percent in 2015.

Construction and Real Estate

Commercial construction activity increased. Recent industry reports noted increased interest in building new hotels across many parts of the District. In Sioux Falls, S.D., the value of January commercial permits increased from a year ago. In Billings, Mont., commercial permits decreased in value in January from a year earlier. Residential construction activity in the District was down compared with a year ago. In the Minneapolis-St. Paul area, the value of January residential permits decreased 19 percent compared with January 2014. The value of January residential permits in Sioux Falls decreased from a year earlier. However, January residential building permits in Billings increased in value from the previous year.

Activity in commercial real estate markets increased since the previous report. A commercial real estate broker noted recent increases in sales and leasing transactions in the Minneapolis-St. Paul area. A real estate firm expected increased absorption and sales prices of industrial buildings in the Fargo, N.D., area in 2015 compared with last year. Residential real estate market activity was mixed. Minnesota home sales were down 9 percent in January from a year earlier, the inventory of homes for sale increased 1 percent, and the median sales price rose 10 percent. In the Sioux Falls area, January home sales were up 5 percent, inventory decreased 4 percent, and the median sales price increased 8 percent relative to a year earlier.

Services

Activity at professional business services firms increased since the previous report. Merger and acquisition services firms noted increased consulting activity. A large oil-drilling services company noted recent reduced demand due to lower oil prices. A railroad recently announced plans to increase capital expenditures in several District states.

Manufacturing

Manufacturing activity increased since the previous report. A manufacturing index released by Creighton University (Omaha, Neb.) increased in January from the previous month in North Dakota and South Dakota, but it fell slightly in Minnesota. The index remained at levels consistent with expansion in activity in all three states. A manufacturer of capital equipment reported that demand in January was stronger than expected.

Energy and Mining

The energy and mining sectors contracted since the last report. Oil and gas exploration activity fell rapidly in response to lower prices; the number of active drilling rigs in North Dakota and Montana fell to 128 in mid-February compared with 179 at the beginning of the year. An investor contact reported less interest in funding renewable energy technologies, due to cheaper fuel. A Montana copper-silver mine will be idled in response to low metals prices. However, a clay mine in Montana applied for a permit to expand. Production at District iron ore mines is expected to be slightly higher in 2015 than last year.

Agriculture

On balance, District agricultural conditions were down, with livestock and dairy producers faring better than crop farmers. According to preliminary results from the Minneapolis Fed's fourth-quarter (January) survey of agricultural credit conditions, 70 percent of respondents said farm incomes had fallen from a year earlier, while 73 percent reported decreases in capital spending; the first-quarter outlook was similar. Land values and rents fell in 2014 in Minnesota and North Dakota, according to appraisers.

Employment, Wages, and Prices

While labor markets continued to tighten in several areas, signs of loosening were noted in the energy-producing region. Business owners in South Dakota noted difficulty finding workers to fill openings for skilled construction and manufacturing positions. In western Montana, business owners in several sectors noted difficulty finding qualified workers. A Minnesota staffing firm reported that finding workers was difficult and that competition for those workers increased recently. A representative of a Minnesota information technology firm noted relatively low worker turnover despite the strength in the sector. However, a retailer in Minnesota announced 550 job cuts, and a plant that salvages electronics parts closed, affecting almost 80 jobs.

Decreased oil- and gas-drilling activity in western North Dakota and eastern Montana has led to reduced hours and layoffs of oilfield workers. The number of job postings in the region has also decreased, but several companies in a variety of sectors are still looking for employees. Businesses in and around the energy-producing region have noticed an increase in the number of job applicants for open positions.

While wage pressures in the energy-producing region moderated, wage pressures rose in other areas, as reports of wage increases above 3 percent were noted more frequently during the past couple months. Nevertheless, wage increases generally remained moderate.

Price pressures were subdued, as oil and gasoline prices decreased during January. Minnesota gasoline prices in mid-February were over a dollar per gallon lower than a year ago. Copper prices decreased since the previous report.

TENTH DISTRICT - KANSAS CITY

The Tenth District economy continued to grow slightly in January and early February, and most contacts remained optimistic about future activity. Consumer spending was flat, with a rise in auto and restaurant sales offsetting a decrease in retail and tourism activity. District manufacturing and other business activity rose as increases in transportation, professional, high-tech services, and wholesale trade activity outweighed small declines in overall manufacturing production. Real estate activity increased slightly, and both commercial and residential inventories declined further. Banking contacts reported mixed loan demand across sectors, stable loan quality, and steady deposit levels. District farm income and crop prices decreased, cropland values remained steady, and ranchland values increased compared to the previous survey period. Energy activity continued to slow and was expected to fall further. Prices continued to grow modestly, and wages grew slightly since the previous survey period. A few contacts noted a short supply of workers for truck drivers, management, skilled technicians, and IT developers.

Consumer Spending. Consumer spending activity was flat in January and early February, but remained higher than a year ago with solid expectations for the coming months. Retail sales declined from the previous survey but were around year-ago levels. Several retailers noted a drop in sales of luxury products, although sales of winter and lower-priced items were steady. Expectations for future sales were increasingly positive, and inventory levels were expected to remain fairly stable. Auto sales rebounded in January and early February, particularly for trucks, and dealer contacts expected moderate growth in the months ahead. Auto inventories rose from the previous survey period, with additional increases expected. Restaurant sales improved modestly and were considerably above year-ago levels, with positive growth expected in the coming months. District tourism activity remained sluggish, although activity was higher than a year ago. Contacts in Colorado, however, reported strong tourism activity compared to the previous survey period and expected further gains over the coming months.

Manufacturing and Other Business Activity. Overall District manufacturing activity expanded at a slow pace in January and early February, while other business activity increased. Despite a slight decrease in manufacturing production since the previous survey, inventories and supplier delivery times rose and producers' expectations for future activity remained solid. Slower growth was mostly attributable to declines in some types of durable goods production, particularly electronics, machinery, and metal products, some of which was likely due to lower energy activity.

In contrast, nondurable goods producers reported a slight increase in production, especially for food and plastics products. Looking across District states, the weakest factory activity was in energy-dependent Oklahoma. Manufacturers' capital spending plans were not as strong as in the previous survey, but hiring plans remained solid. Transportation firms reported stronger activity, and sales were above year-ago levels with solid expectations for future months. Professional, high-tech services, and wholesale trade contacts also noted a slight increase in sales from the previous survey, but the pace of growth was expected to slow slightly in coming months. Most firms reported solid growth in capital spending plans.

Real Estate and Construction. District real estate activity increased slightly as moderate growth in commercial real estate activity was partially offset by modest declines in residential real estate sales. Residential sales decreased modestly since the previous survey, partially due to typical seasonal sales patterns and low inventories. Sales of low- and medium-priced homes continued to outpace sales of higher-priced homes. Home prices made strong gains, and inventories continued to decline. Expectations for sales and prices remained positive, and inventories were expected to fall further. Residential construction activity was flat in January and early February. Builders and construction supply contacts expected moderate growth in residential real estate activity in the coming months supported by higher home prices, sales, and starts. Commercial real estate activity continued to rise moderately as vacancy rates decreased and absorption increased at a faster pace. Growth in commercial real estate completions, sales, prices, and construction underway slowed slightly, but remained positive. The commercial real estate market was expected to continue to strengthen at a moderate pace in the months ahead.

Banking. Bankers reported mixed loan demand across sectors in January and early February, while loan quality and deposit levels were stable. Respondents indicated increased demand for residential real estate loans, and demand for commercial and industrial and consumer installment loans was mostly steady. However, respondents reported a slight decrease in demand for agricultural loans. Most bankers indicated loan quality was unchanged compared to a year ago, while a slight majority of bankers expected the outlook for loan quality to improve over the next six months. Credit standards remained largely unchanged in all major loan categories. In addition, deposit levels were stable for a majority of bankers.

Agriculture. District farm income weakened further since the last survey period, but cropland values generally held steady. Corn and soybean prices edged down in January and early

February, and farm income remained well below year-ago levels even as profitability in the livestock sector remained relatively strong. After several years of herd culling, District cattle operators retained more replacement heifers compared with last year, indicating the potential for rebuilding herds in 2015. Following several years of strong gains, District non-irrigated and irrigated cropland values leveled off while ranchland values continued to rise due to strong demand for good-quality pasture. Lower farm income trimmed farm loan repayment rates and increased demand for new loans as well as loan renewals and extensions. Looking forward, District contacts expected modest declines in cropland values and further deterioration in farm loan repayment rates amid tighter profit margins for crop producers.

Energy. Energy activity in the District continued to slow and oil and gas producers attempted to reduce costs in January and early February as a result of low oil prices. The number of active oil and gas drilling rigs fell sharply through early February. Many producers reported large capital spending cuts and several announced layoffs. Future drilling activity was expected to fall, and to increasingly focus on core areas. Additionally, respondents commented that cash flows would determine future capital spending levels. Contacts expected oilfield activity to become more efficient with cost reductions, thus limiting declines in oil production. Natural gas spot prices remained stable but low despite typical seasonally cold temperatures across the nation this winter.

Wages and Prices. Compared to the previous survey period, prices continued to increase modestly in most industries. Wages also continued to rise slightly, with some respondents noting sustained shortages of certain workers. Retail prices rose modestly as input prices continued to grow at a moderate pace. Restaurant menu prices maintained their modest growth rate. Manufacturers' raw materials prices increased at a slower rate than in the previous survey. Finished goods prices held steady, but were moderately higher than a year ago. Transportation contacts reported moderately lower input prices, but selling prices edged higher. Construction materials prices rose over the survey period and were expected to continue to increase. Wages continued to grow moderately in the retail, restaurant, and transportation sectors, but were expected to grow at a slightly faster rate moving forward. Some contacts cited labor shortages, especially for truck drivers, management, skilled technicians, and IT developers.

ELEVENTH DISTRICT—DALLAS

The Eleventh District economy expanded at roughly the same pace as in the prior reporting period. Manufacturing activity was mostly stable or increased, but there were a few reports of decreased activity. Retailers and auto dealers reported higher sales. Demand for business and transportation services was mixed. Home sales continued on an upward trend and apartment demand remained strong, but office leasing activity held steady or slowed. Demand for oilfield services declined sharply, while agricultural conditions and loan demand improved slightly. Upward price and wage pressures continued to moderate. Employment in most industries held steady or increased. Overall expectations for the future were generally positive, but contacts expressed uncertainty and caution in their outlooks.

Prices   Most responding firms said prices held steady or declined over the past six weeks. Manufacturers generally reported stable selling prices, and flat to lower input costs. Retailers and auto dealers noted steady prices, and accounting and legal firms said billing rates were unchanged since the prior report. Airlines reported lower fees and airfares, and transportation service firms noted declining fuel costs. In contrast, most staffing firms said they had raised billing rates to offset higher costs associated with the Affordable Care Act. Fabricated metals manufacturers noted continued but slower growth in prices, and one transportation service firm reported higher rates.

The decline in the price of West Texas Intermediate crude oil abated toward the end of the reporting period. Natural gas prices mostly remained below $3, despite harsh winter weather in the North East. Gasoline prices rose moderately in the latter part of the reporting period, while on-highway diesel prices and chemical and polymer product prices declined.

Labor Market   Employment in most industries held steady or increased. Retailers and auto dealers noted stable employment levels, while manufacturers noted flat to increased employment. A few staffing, financial and transportation services firms reported increased payrolls, and construction contacts continued to report a tight labor market. Accounting firms said they hired new classes of interns for the tax season, and added that many of them will transition into fulltime jobs. Law firms noted increased competition for top law students, and staffing firms noted strong demand for IT professionals. Energy firms said they have halted hiring and started downsizing, with most expecting payrolls to decline in the first half of the year. Two firms in the retail sector said it was easier to find workers in areas near the oil fields.

Reports of rising wage pressures were less prevalent than in the prior report. Staffing services firms noted little to no wage pressure, and petrochemical manufacturers reported reduced wage pressure, particularly for downstream construction workers. High-tech manufacturers reported continued wage pressures for high skilled positions, particularly in areas with strong growth and low unemployment. Law firms said hiring of Texas lawyers by out-of-state firms establishing practices in Texas had increased wage pressure in the industry.

Manufacturing   Overall manufacturing activity was flat to up, but there were some reports of weaker demand. Construction-related manufacturers reported mixed demand. Cement producers saw a slight dip in orders over the reporting period, which one firm attributed to lower oil prices, while brick and primary metals manufacturers noted stable demand. Fabricated metals firms saw slower growth in sales compared with the prior report, and said demand was well below year-ago levels.

Demand for high-tech manufacturing increased since the last report, with orders for electronic devices growing at a good pace and demand for memory chips remaining very strong. Inventories were at desired levels, and the outlook for the next six months was for continued moderate to strong growth. Food producers saw a modest increase in demand, and remained largely positive in their outlooks. Transportation and machinery manufacturers noted flat to higher demand, with the exception of an oil-field machinery manufacturing firm, which reported a sharp drop in bookings since the prior report.

Gulf Coast chemical producers reported declining export demand. Refinery utilization rates, while still high, decreased slightly in January. Contacts said low oil prices have reduced production growth expectations, resulting in some midstream construction projects being delayed. Outlooks remained positive and margins healthy, although the refining side of the business was more profitable than chemicals.

Retail Sales   Retail sales rose during the reporting period, but the pace of growth was mixed. Demand continued to be up year over year, and a few retailers noted slight improvement in foot traffic since the last report. Two national retailers said Texas' sales performance was in line with the nation overall, while a third national retailer noted Texas was outperforming the national average. Outlooks were positive, and contacts expect modest sales growth over the next three months.

Automobile sales increased over the reporting period, and demand was higher than a year ago. Contacts expect steady demand growth over the first quarter, but reported more uncertainty in their outlooks for the remainder of the year.

Nonfinancial Services   Demand for staffing services was flat to higher, and outlooks were positive, but much more cautious than the last report. Two firms said that strength in demand had shifted slightly away from Houston, which is more affected by energy activity, toward Dallas-Fort Worth, while a third noted a pullback in demand from the oil and gas sector. The accounting sector saw a seasonal increase in activity. Abstracting from seasonal movements, accounting services to auto dealerships was strong, and demand from clients in private medical practice, food services and construction industries held steady. In contrast, low oil prices stalled some projects, and tax advisory work in Houston slowed. Overall demand for legal services held steady, but contacts in Houston noted a slight decline. Litigation and bankruptcy work picked up, but transaction work for law firm offices in Houston slowed moderately. Demand for real estate-related work continued to do well, although Houston showed signs of slowing.

Changes in cargo volumes were mixed, and outlooks of transportation service firms were mostly positive. Trucking firms said cargo volumes declined because of shipping disruptions at West Coast ports, while rail and small-parcel shipments increased in January, and were up year over year. Container traffic trended upwards, largely driven by strength in the Asian and Transatlantic markets. Airlines said passenger demand weakened, particularly to South American markets, and outlooks were slightly less optimistic.

Construction and Real Estate Housing activity remained solid, and outlooks were mostly positive. Home sales rose during the reporting period, although reports on the pace of growth were mixed. Contacts in Dallas-Fort Worth noted a strong, earlier-than-normal pickup in traffic and sales, while demand in Houston held steady. Home prices continued to edge upward. Land prices were elevated, and several contacts reported decreased builders' appetite for land. Apartment demand stayed strong, particularly for class B space. Rent growth remained solid in Dallas-Fort Worth, but slowed in Houston.

Commercial real estate activity held steady or slowed since the previous report, and outlooks were cautiously optimistic. Overall office leasing activity remained fairly solid; however, contacts said some energy firms are seeking to sublet office space in Houston. Institutional equity for new development has nearly dried up in Houston, and a few projects have been put on hold or cancelled.

Financial Services Loan demand increased slightly over the past six weeks. Growth in consumer lending remained robust, and commercial real estate, as well as construction and industrial lending, continued to provide a healthy pipeline of work. The quality of loans previously made to oil and gas firms remained high, although contacts expressed concern about the future because of low oil prices. Deposit volumes grew over the reporting period, despite expectations for a slight seasonal decrease. Outlooks were optimistic, but more cautious compared with the previous report. Interest rates on loans remained at historically low levels, and deposit rates continued to hover just above zero.

Energy Demand for oilfield services fell sharply in the Eleventh District. Declines were concentrated in the Permian Basin and Eagle Ford regions, and contacts reported a pullback in both horizontal and traditional vertical drilling. Outlooks remain pessimistic and uncertain, with firms expecting a roughly 30 percent decline in capital expenditures this year.

Agriculture Moisture conditions stabilized for a large portion of the District, but drought conditions persisted in some areas. Cotton prices are below profitable levels for most producers. Prices and export demand for sorghum is high, which may lead more farmers to favor sorghum over cotton when making planting decisions this spring. The strong dollar has slowed agricultural exports. Corn, cattle, wheat, soybeans and dairy prices declined over the reporting period.

TWELFTH DISTRICT–SAN FRANCISCO

Summary

Economic activity in the Twelfth District continued to improve moderately during the reporting period of early January through mid-February. Overall price inflation remained modest, while wage inflation was moderate. Retail sales and demand for business and consumer services increased moderately. Overall manufacturing activity picked up, while agricultural conditions were mixed. Real estate activity advanced, mainly in the multifamily construction sector. Lending activity increased modestly.

Prices and Wages

Overall price inflation remained modest during the reporting period. Reports of stable prices were widespread across the District. Several contacts observed that businesses in general appear to be using any decreases in input prices stemming from oil price declines to increase profit margins rather than decrease final prices of their products. However, contacts did note that the fuel surcharge for courier services and for delivery of wood products had declined. The price of sheetrock increased dramatically in some areas during the reporting period. Prices of branded and specialty pharmaceuticals increased markedly. Competition from imports contributed to a dramatic decline in scrap steel prices.

In general, wages increased at a moderate pace during the reporting period. While several contacts reported that wages had increased at about the rate of price inflation in their area, several others noted slightly faster overall wage growth. Wage pressures continued to be relatively strong for various information technology occupations. Contacts submitted scattered reports of increasing labor costs in construction. In some areas, upward wage pressures appeared for certain health-care positions, including registered nurses and pharmacists. Some tourist areas saw intensified bidding for restaurant workers.

Retail Trade and Services

Overall retail sales activity grew moderately during the reporting period. Automobile sales were strong, and demand for SUVs was robust. Some contacts reported new data on holiday sales since the last reporting period. Merchants in some areas showed very strong holiday sales and would have seen even larger volumes if not for delays receiving merchandise caused by labor disputes at West Coast ports. In other regions, holiday sales were not quite as strong as expected, and, as a result, retailers in those areas still have a little excess inventory. Contacts reported that most retailers are optimistic about growth over the coming year, citing decreases in gas prices and improvements in employment conditions. However, the outlook is weaker in areas where unemployment remains relatively high.

Demand for business and consumer services grew moderately during the reporting period. Travel and tourism to Southern California increased compared with the same period a year ago. The number of international casual tourists climbed, and spending was strong in airport duty-free shops, despite the increase in the value of the dollar. Advance hotel bookings from the business segment declined somewhat. Overall travel and tourism activity in Hawaii declined a bit from the same period last year. Contacts from various areas reported that spending at restaurants increased and that new establishments opened. Some contacts observed an increase in physician and hospital visits and surmised that the growth in the number of insured patients under the Affordable Care Act has spurred demand. However, others, citing the growth of high deductible health insurance plans, observed a decline in demand for health care services.

Manufacturing

Overall District manufacturing activity grew moderately. Contacts reported strong energy demand from aerospace, metals, and wood products manufacturers. Biotechnology and pharmaceutical manufacturing earnings were healthy. Orders for and deliveries of commercial aircraft increased in 2014, and 2015 is expected to be a record year for sales. U.S. Department of Defense budget challenges have reduced new orders and diminished capacity utilization in the defense aerospace sector. Reduced demand for equipment used in mining and the energy sector contributed to softening orders for recycled steel and metals. However, demand for these products from the auto industry and the commercial construction sector remained robust.

Agriculture and Resource-Related Industries

Agricultural conditions in the District were mixed during the reporting period. Drought conditions and unseasonably warm weather in parts of the District contributed to lower yields, but the associated increases in many of the prices received by farmers resulted in slightly higher revenues. Farmers remain concerned that the drought will continue, requiring them to leave more acreage fallow. Numerous contacts reported that the labor disputes at West Coast ports reduced agricultural exports, as perishable products such as fruits wasted away in storage containers waiting for shipment. Contacts also stated that the stronger dollar limited exports. Offshore demand for logs, especially from China, slowed, while domestic demand increased slightly.

Real Estate and Construction

Real estate activity advanced during the reporting period. Multifamily residential real estate construction activity remained strong in many areas of the District. Some areas anticipate that single-family home construction will soon pick up, as the pace of building permit issuance has climbed notably. In other areas, the pace of new construction remained slow, and single-family housing inventories continued to drift down. One contact commented that single-family home construction in their area has been limited to only pre-sold homes. In some relatively fast-growing areas, shortages of skilled labor are contributing to the tepid pace of construction. Several contacts reported a pick-up in the pace of single-family home sales but little change in prices. Commercial rents in the San Francisco Bay Area continued to rise even in the face of significant new construction, and rents for restaurant space in the Los Angeles area crept up. In other areas, commercial rents remained stable.

Financial Institutions

Lending activity in the District increased modestly during the reporting period. Demand for commercial real estate loans continued to climb, and demand for agricultural loans picked up. Some contacts reported that demand for small business loans strengthened, with owners beginning to expand and purchase new equipment. Demand for consumer loans other than for autos remained somewhat weak. Some contacts observed that, even with low interest rates, consumers are more cautious about taking on additional debt than at this time last year. Several contacts stated that recent declines in mortgage interest rates contributed to a small wave of refinancing activity. Deposit growth was strong in many areas, and banks have ample liquidity. Stiff competition for high-quality borrowers exerted downward pressure on loan interest rates. Overall credit quality remained good, but some contacts reported that lenders in their area appear willing to relax credit standards to imprudent levels in order to capture customers.

www.ingramcontent.com/pod-product-compliance
Lightning Source LLC
Chambersburg PA
CBHW080615180526
45168CB00007B/2927